what you want

... y ...

DATE DUE

a gu   ho
kr   t

Patricia Hipwell

logonliteracy

UK edition published by Carel Press, office@carelpress.co.uk
www.carelpress.co.uk

Australian edition published by logonliteracy and Boolarong Press

ISBN: 9781925046953

Text and cover design: Watson Ferguson & Company
Editing and proofreading: Jan Maskey

Note: Text examples of the writing skill have been created to demonstrate that skill. Possible inaccuracies and out-of-date information in these texts are acknowledged by the author and do not detract from the validity of their inclusion.

Printed and bound by Interpress, Budapest

contents

dedication

To my daughter, Elizabeth — the inspiration for this book, by being the embodiment of the student who knows what she wants to say but can't always find the words!

introduction

This guide, written by Patricia Hipwell of **logonliteracy**, provides students with the language they need to write for a range of purposes. The book aims to provide students with a starting point to say what they want to say using language that mature writers use.

The book is set out in a double-page format:

- **The first page** defines the **WRITING SKILL** and provides the **SENTENCE STARTERS** to demonstrate that skill.
- **The second page** provides linking words and phrases for **CONNECTING THE IDEAS WITHIN AND BETWEEN SENTENCES;** an **EXAMPLE** of the **SKILL** in a short piece of writing; and the **KEY TASK WORDS** linked to the **SKILL**.

How to write what you want to say: a guide for those students who know what they want to say but can't find the words provides parents, teachers and students with a unique tool for improving writing. It suits students from Year 7 to university level.

key terms and ideas defined

writing skill	the purpose of writing; includes such purposes as describing, comparing, evaluating, justifying
sentence starter	the opening clause of a sentence
key task words	words in questions that establish what is required in the answer
formal language	language that is more characteristic of how we write than how we speak; does not contain colloquialisms or slang; adheres to the conventions of print—grammar, spelling and punctuation are correct
linking words and phrases	these connect ideas within sentences or ideas from one sentence to the next
modality	expressing ideas such as possibility, certainty, frequency and importance using additional words to extend the main verb.

analysing

meaning:

the process of examining the parts of something in detail and discussing or interpreting the relationship of the parts to each other and to the whole; may involve description, comparison, explanation, interpretation and critical comment

mathematics meaning:

using statistical techniques to summarise, compare or infer something

sentence starters

………. could be broken down in the following way/s:

The issue of ………. can be viewed from several different perspectives.

The main similarities/differences between ………. and ………. are ……….

If ………. were changed, then the problem/issue/event/experiment would be affected in the following ways:

………. would happen if ………. was/were changed.

………. effectively combines ………. and ……….

The actions of ………. enable us to understand ……….

Missing from the text is the ………. (view/perspective/opinion, etc.) of ……….

There is a complex relationship between ………. and ……….

………. is a fact because ………., whereas ………. is an opinion because ……….

There is a strong connection between ………. and ……….

………. is composed of/combines with ……….

In the case of ………., the following details have emerged:

There is very little relationship between ………. and ……….

All of the features of ………. contribute to ……….

In the first/second/third instance, ……….

………. means that ……….

linking words and phrases

although	by	for instance	in the same way	than
and	comprises	furthermore	is made up of	thus
and this/that	consists of	however	is similar to/ different from	unless
as well as	differ/different	if … then	on the other hand	when … then …
because	even if	in addition	provides	which is/allows/ gives
for as long as	for example	in other respects	some	yet

example

The iPod Nano **effectively merges** two approaches to music storage *and this* makes it significantly *different* from its competitors. **The iPod Nano's tiny hard drive, which offers huge capacity, is combined** with a memory chip *which allows* for a more compact design. The iPod Nano's memory chips are incredibly small *yet* their four gigabyte capacity matches that of some hard drive players — the equivalent of 1000 songs. **The absence of moving parts means that** the iPod Nano is less delicate *than* full sized iPods *and* unlikely to skip.

The high resolution colour screen *provides* sharp images *which give* stunning clarity to album-cover art, photo collections *and* the menu system. Navigation is made simple *by* the click-wheel scrolling device *and this* permits quick access to any one of the 1000 stored songs. The iPod Nano is light-weight and, *even if* it is dropped, the ear bud cord catches it. **All of the features of the iPod Nano contribute to** the appeal of this personal music player and ensure that it will be popular amongst lovers of personal music players everywhere.

key task words

see glossary pp. 44-47
- describe
- analyse
- compare
- synthesise
- interpret
- break down
- distinguish

arguing/persuading

meaning:

presenting one or both sides of an argument and using persuasive techniques to convince others that your opinion about something is the correct one

sentence starters

Nothing polarises opinion in quite the same way as the issue of ………

In recent years opinion has become much more divided on the issue of ………

(State point of view). There are several very convincing arguments to support this point of view.

Firstly, let us consider the argument that ………—easy to state but difficult to substantiate.

The issue of ……… is highly controversial because ………

There has been much debate about ………

The main objection to the alternatives is ………

It is necessary to consider ………

In spite of/Despite this ………

To argue ……… is insufficient; it fails to consider………

Ultimately it must be realised that ………

All the evidence points conclusively to ………

……… has/have been vehemently opposed to ………

There is a great deal of evidence to support ………, not least of which is ………

The evidence that supports this argument is accurate/credible/reliable/unreliable/difficult to substantiate.

It is difficult to decide whether or not ………

(State point of view) Whilst there are several convincing arguments that support this point of view, the balance of the argument is weighted in favour of ………

It would appear that the issue of ……… is quite straightforward; however, closer inspection reveals compelling arguments both in favour and against ………

However, if we are to come to a conclusion, we must consider both points of view.

linking words and phrases

absolutely	finally	in conclusion	on the other hand	therefore, it seems likely that
admittedly	furthermore	inevitable/ inevitably	one reason for	this/that
at one level	hence	moreover	so	ultimately
because	however	nevertheless	such as	whilst
beyond doubt	if … then	obvious/obviously	there are many reasons	without question
even though evidence suggests	in addition	of course	therefore	

example

An orgy of unrestrained hunting has already sent many species of whales to the brink of extinction. **Nothing polarises opinion globally in quite the same way as the issue** of whaling. **However, if we are** to ensure the survival of these amazing creatures, *then* commercial whaling must cease immediately. *This* can only happen *if* countries *that* continue to ignore the opposition of the rest of the world receive much harsher penalties. Environmental groups have often been powerless in the face of the scale of whaling and the difficulty of locating whalers. *Without question*, whale numbers of some species have plummeted dramatically since the beginning of the 19th century.

Whaling is a highly controversial issue. Countries such as Japan and Iceland have killed whales in the name of science, *even though* the meat that they take ends up on the dinner tables of their fancy 5 star restaurants. *However*, countries *such as* Australia and New Zealand **have been vehemently opposed** to the senseless slaughter of these beautiful creatures for many decades.

key task words

see glossary pp. 44-47

- argue
- comment on
- expound
- propose
- construct
- debate
- quote
- exemplify
- justify
- illustrate
- suggest
- state

classifying

sentence starters

Based on ...., the following items can be grouped together like this:

This heading/These headings provides/provide a suitable classification for ....

The following classification has been developed for ....

In this group, the following have several attributes in common and these include ....

This is a very large group; therefore sub-categories can be created.

A, B and C have the trait of ....; therefore they can be grouped.

Common to all of these is the characteristic of ....

.... can be included in this group because it/he/she/they has/have .... in common with the other members of the group.

The following are alike according to the criteria of ....

There are two categories of .... and these are ....

The criterion/criteria for inclusion in this group is/are ....

Despite the superficial characteristic/s of ...., this item/product merits inclusion in the category of ....

Inclusion in this category is possible because .... has the characteristic of ....

.... is the odd one out in this category because ....

The following have the attribute/attributes of .... in common:

The inclusion of .... can be defended by ....

.... can be classified as .... On the other hand, ... can be classified as ....

There are clear differences between .... and ....; therefore they belong in different categories.

For the most part, the items in this group have common characteristics which include ....

The proposed solutions can be sorted into short-term and long-term ones.

linking words and phrases

and therefore	for the most part	in general	normally	there are examples
and these are	generally	in most cases	on average	typically
associated with	if	in many cases	on the other hand	usually
because	in all cases	mainly	so	while
commonly	in all instances	many	such as	whilst
except	in common	mostly	tend to be	without exception

example

There are two categories of timber and these are hardwoods and softwoods. _Whilst_ it is tempting to believe that hardwoods are hard and dense and softwoods light and easier to cut, **the criterion for inclusion in either group** is based on what they have _in common_ in terms of their reproduction. **Timber can be classified as hardwood** _if_ it comes from a tree that is an angiosperm. Angiosperms are plants that produce seeds with some type of covering, _such as_ a shell or fruit. _On the other hand_, softwoods are gymnosperms and their seeds fall to the ground and quickly germinate _because_ they have no covering.

Balsawood can be included in the hardwood category _because_, even though it is a light wood of low density, it comes from a tree that is a gymnosperm.

For the most part, angiosperms lose their leaves in the cold weather and gymnosperms retain their leaves all year round, _so_ it is reasonable to say that deciduous trees are hardwoods and evergreen trees are softwoods. **The hardwood/softwood classification** does make some sense, though. Evergreens _tend to be_ less dense than deciduous trees, _and therefore_ easier to cut, _whilst_ most hardwoods are stronger and more dense. **But, as the classification of balsawood shows,** _there are examples_ of hardwoods that are light.

key task words

see glossary pp. 44-47

- classify
- categorise
- sort
- arrange
- define
- differentiate
- discriminate
- distinguish

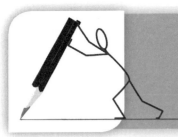

comparing

meaning:

examining two or more things and noting the ways in which they are similar **AND** different

sentence starters

There are several ways in which A and B are similar, including ……….

The main difference between A and B is ……….

The most striking similarity between A and B is ……….

Obvious differences exist between A and B, particularly the fact that ……….

This differs from ……….

There are differences of opinion between ……….

Closer inspection reveals that, whilst A and B appear very similar, subtle differences exist.

………. and ………. have more in common than ………. and ………., especially the fact that ………

………. and ………. are similar because they both are/have ……….

………. and ………. are different because ………. is ……….; however, ………. is ……….

The elements of ………. and ………. will be compared.

The similarities between A and B are insignificant when compared with their differences.

A comparison of ………. and ………. reveals noteworthy and highly significant differences.

This is similar to ……….

The features of ………. and ………. are similar, whereas the features of ………. and ………. are different.

Initially, there were no differences between ………. and ………. but, as time progressed, significant differences emerged.

Just as ………. is/are ………., so ………. is/are ……….

In so many ways, A and B are similar, and yet these are often forgotten as the differences are given prominence.

Specific differences exist between ………. and ……….

The similarities between ………. and ………. are more relevant than the differences.

linking words and phrases

alike/like/just like	but	in contrast to	nevertheless	similar in that
also	compared with/ by comparison	in other respects	not only ... but also	similarly
alternative/ alternatively	concurrent/ concurrently	in spite of this	on the contrary	specifically
although	differs from	in the same way	on the one hand	the way that
as well as	even though	just as ... so ...	on the other hand	whereas
both/in both/all cases	however	more/greater than	rather	x is similar to y

example

ARE SPORTS DRINKS BETTER THAN WATER?

Sports drinks have become very popular in recent years and advertisers promote their benefits. Are they much better for you than water? **A comparison of the two drinks** reveals a few facts of which consumers should be aware. **The most striking similarity between** sports drinks and water is that they _both_ hydrate the body. _However_, sports drinks contain kilojoules which need to be burnt, or they are stored as fat in the body, and _this differs from_ water, which contains no kilojoules. _Both_ sports drinks and water cost money—if you buy bottled water—_but_ tap water is inexpensive _by comparison_. The major difference is that sports drinks contain significant amounts of sugar that can cause tooth decay, _whereas_ water helps to maintain healthy teeth by washing away a build-up of bacteria after eating or drinking.

Water is absorbed very quickly by the body. **This differs from** the rate of absorption of sports drinks, which is longer and can, therefore, give an energy boost for events lasting longer than 60 minutes. Sports drinks contain electrolytes, which replace the salts lost when sweating; _alternatively_, water does not contain electrolytes.

key task words

see glossary pp. 44-47

- compare
- contrast
- differentiate
- distinguish

concluding

meaning:

drawing together the main ideas of something and restating them in a succinct way, often as a decision; a conclusion may involve making recommendations for the future

sentence starters

A conclusion can be drawn from ……….

Thus, to conclude/in conclusion ……….

Clearly, it can be concluded that ……….

It would appear reasonable to conclude that ………. and, therefore, recommend ……….

On balance, it would seem that the main conclusion is ……….

There is, therefore, some doubt that this is the best conclusion.

There is absolutely no doubt that this is the most valid conclusion.

Consequently, it would seem better to ………. than ……….

To sum up, then, ……….

Audiences everywhere will enjoy this performance of ……….

Considering all the options, it would seem better to ……….

It is appropriate now to make some concluding remarks/observations.

All things considered, the following conclusion can be stated:

The conclusion is by no means clear; however, ……….

An examination of all the data allows the following conclusions to be drawn:

The arguments discussed conclusively support the point of view that ……….

There is general agreement that ……….

These are the final statements made here to support ……….

Thus, in summary, ……….

An examination of the evidence allows the following summary to be made:

linking words and phrases

accordingly	clearly	in any case	now	the final point
all things considered	conclusively	in summary	on balance	then
although	consequently	inconclusively	on condition that	these/which include
as a final point	decisive/decisively	inevitable/ inevitably	overwhelming/ overwhelmingly	thus
assuming that	finally	much doubt	so	to conclude
because	if	no doubt	some doubt	we can conclude

example

Clearly, it can be concluded that international travellers who follow all the guidelines outlined in this information leaflet will enjoy a safe and happy experience overseas. **There is no doubt** that the precautions and preparation taken prior to travel, _which include_ taking out travel insurance and checking out the latest travel advice for your destination, are essential. **The weight of evidence** suggests that travellers who flout local laws in the countries they visit cannot be guaranteed the protection of the British Government.

As a final point, travellers should ensure that all relevant paperwork (passports, visas, travel documentation, itineraries, etc.) is up to date and photocopied. It is preferable to register all travel and contact details online.

key task words

see glossary pp. 44-47

- conclude
- summarise
- investigate
- deduce
- examine

contrasting

sentence starters

The main differences between ………. and ………. are ……….

………. and ………. have nothing in common; only differences are apparent.

Obvious differences exist between A and B, particularly the fact that ……….

This differs from ……….

There are differences of opinion about ……….

………. and ………. are different because ………. is ………., whereas ………. is ……….

Initially, there were no differences between ………. and ………. However, as time progressed significant
differences emerged.

Specific differences exist between ………. and ……….

The elements of ………. and ………. are very different.

Subtle differences exist between ………. and ……….

Whilst ………. is like ………., ………. is like ……….

Slight differences appeared at first and these became more noticeable over time.

………. and ………. have far less in common than would at first appear.

The distinguishing characteristics of ………. make it very different from anything else.

Be careful not to overlook the hidden differences between ………. and ……….

………. and ………. are not alike in any way.

A comparison of ………. and ………. reveals only differences.

………. is at variance with ……….

There is nothing about ………. and ………. that is in any way similar.

………. is dissimilar from ……….

………. is not like ………. in any way.

linking words and phrases

admittedly	even so	in other respects	on the contrary	rather
alternatively	even though	in spite of this	on the one hand	unlike
although	however	more/greater than	on the other hand	whereas
by contrast	in contrast	nevertheless	opposing	while
conversely	in fact	no commonality	or	whilst
differs from	in no way similar	not only ... but also	other differences	yet

example

Specific differences exist between plant and animal cells. Animal cells are round and irregular in shape. **This differs from** plant cells, which are a rectangular and fixed shape.

Whilst plant cells contain chloroplasts to enable them to make their own food, animal cells do not. **Animal cells are dissimilar** from plant cells in that they have a cell wall and a cell membrane, *whereas* plant cells have only the cell membrane. Cilia are present in animal cells; *in contrast* they are rare in plant cells.

One or more small vacuoles exist in animal cells; *however*, plant cells contain one large central vacuole which takes up 90% of the cell volume. Liposomes occur in the cytoplasm of animal cells. *On the other hand*, they are usually not evident in the cytoplasm of plant cells.

key task words

see glossary pp. 44-47

- contrast
- differentiate
- distinguish

describing

meaning:
giving a detailed account of the properties/
qualities/features/parts of something or someone

sentence starters

One of the characteristics of ………. is ……….

………. has a number of distinguishing/special/notable features, including ……….

The key features of ………. are ……….

………. looks /sounds/feels/tastes/smells like ……….

An examination of ………. reveals ……….

………. has several distinguishing features, which include ……….

The major attribute of ………. is ……….

………. has some distinctive features/characteristics which make it unique.

………. comprises/is composed of/consists of/is constructed of ……….

Other important aspects include ……….

The most significant elements of ………. include ……….

………. has some very distinctive traits especially ……….

………. is unlike anything else seen/experienced previously, although ……….

A cursory glance reveals several strengths/weaknesses.

Upon examination, it is seen that ……….

This shows that ……….

The most obvious feature of ………. is ……….

The flaws/strengths stand out when ……….

Most prominent is ……….

Other less important features are ……….

Important though ………. is, it is not the most relevant factor in the description.

linking words and phrases

additionally	apart from	extra features	is composed of	shows
all	as shown in/by	for example	mainly	some
along with	as well as	furthermore	moreover	such as
also	besides	however	not only ... but also	the following characteristics
although	combines	in addition	rather than	too
and	extra	include	several	what's more

example

Historically, the Goth scene grew out of the post-Punk movement of the late 1970s. **One of the characteristics of the Goth movement is that** its followers dress **in a distinctive way.** They usually have black hair, with males wearing their hair long. Goths dress predominantly in black and heavy jewellery is worn, often in body piercings. **Important though the appearance of Goths is, it is not the most relevant factor** in describing them.

Being a Goth is more about ways of seeing the world *rather than* outward appearances. Goths are accepting of death *as well as* being preoccupied with the mysterious and supernatural. **Other distinctive traits** *include* moodiness *and* introspection, which may lead to depression, either genuine or fake. *In addition*, Goths tend to be non-violent, *although* they may have a distaste for authority *and* resist it.

Other less important features of Goths include their musical tastes which tend to lean towards heavy rock. *Furthermore*, being Goth means attending concerts with other Goths and generally preferring to 'hang out' with members of the sub-culture. Many Goths are attention seekers and like to shock. *However*, as society's tolerance of difference has increased, many people are no longer shocked by Goths' appearances and behaviours.

key task words

see glossary pp. 44-47

- define
- describe
- identify
- state

elaborating

meaning:
giving more information or more detail about something

sentence starters

Close scrutiny reveals ……….

A detailed examination shows ……….

Careful observation reveals ……….

The information is accurate and supported by evidence, especially the fact that ……….

………. supports the interpretation of the facts, which is ……….

………. attests to the relevance of the information.

Under these circumstances, ………. would apply.

One interpretation of the findings could be ……….

If the topic is placed under the microscope, then it becomes clear that ……….

There is more to the topic/issue than at first appears; therefore, it should be looked at deeply.

At a glance ………. is evident; however, a closer look reveals ……….

One interpretation could be ……….

At one level, ………. is clearly identified, but there is much more to discuss ……….

Looking more closely, it is apparent that ……….

A cursory glance shows ……….; however, closer inspection reveals ……….

There are more details to be examined and these include:

In addition to what is visible, there are other aspects worthy of discussion.

The diagram provides additional information to the text, especially as it shows ……….

linking words and phrases

additionally	besides	for this reason	indicates	specially
albeit	clearly	furthermore	interprets	specifically
also	closely	given this fact	it becomes clear	such as
and so	examines	if ... then ...	it's clear	supports
apparently	for example, (e.g.,)	in addition	moreover	thus
as revealed by	for instance	in detail	reveals	under these circumstances

example

A sophisticated and well developed vocabulary is the hallmark of an educated and highly literate person. *Given this fact*, how do we learn new words and add them to our lexical reservoir? **There is more to this issue of** vocabulary development than first appears. **A cursory glance at** common practices in schools where, one would imagine, the majority of new words are learned, reveals the oft-used practice of looking words up in the dictionary and putting them in sentences. **Under these circumstances**, vocabulary development stalls. Looking a word up in a dictionary is unlikely to encourage students to remember or use the word. The word has to be linked to relevant examples; the examples need to be visualised; and, specifically, students should be encouraged to come up with their own examples of the word in use. *If* students trawl the Internet, *then* they will find examples of words used in unusual ways; *for example*, 'She smelled as though she had spent hours marinating in cheap perfume.' *Besides* these practices, students should study antonyms, synonyms, related words and hypernyms, *which are* more generic versions of words being learnt *e.g.*, vehicle for car. Students who use these practices know more words when they are reading and use more words when writing **and this attests to the relevance of this information**.

key task words

see glossary pp. 44-47

- evaluate
- expand
- interpret
- exemplify
- review
- illustrate
- justify

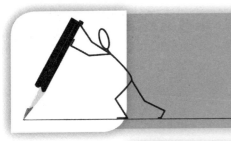

evaluating

meaning:
considering something or someone to make a judgment of value or worth; often this is supported with evidence

mathematics meaning:
finding the exact value of something

sentence starters

………. is a more suitable choice/option/solution because ……….

Despite the criticism of ………., it is a viable alternative.

………. is better/more effective/more appealing/more enjoyable than ……….

………. evokes a feeling of ………. on the one hand, mixed with feelings of ……… on the other.

An examination of the options reveals that ……….

If ………. is compared with ………., several differences emerge and these include ……….

There are significant advantages/disadvantages with ……….

To improve the effectiveness of ………., several changes need to be made, which include …….

The appeal of ………. lies in ……….

The worst feature of ………. is ………. because ……….

………. is worth considering because ……….

The following criteria will be used to evaluate the idea/proposal/scheme/product:

The most outstanding performance was by ………. as he/she/they ……….

Even though parts of ………. are weak, the overall effect is stunning/impressive/memorable/etc.

………. is/was particularly effective because ……….

There are several flaws in the argument and these include ……….

………. is more suitable/logical/ethical/appropriate, etc., than ……….

Some would argue that ……….

There are strengths, on the one hand, and significant flaws on the other.

However, the appeal of the performance/artwork lies in the way the elements have been combined to make powerful statements.

It worked reasonably well when ……….; however, ………. was especially effective.

linking words and phrases

although	by contrast	greater/fewer	in spite of this	therefore
albeit	despite this/the fact that	hence	more/less	thus
apart from	effective/ ineffective	however	nevertheless	when ... then ...
because of this	especially	if ... then ...	on the other hand	whereas
better/worse	for example	in other respects	regardless	while/whilst
by comparison	furthermore	in particular	the effect of	with regard to

example

Best-selling Canadian author, Malcolm Gladwell has delighted readers all over the world with his books that are liberally peppered with the findings of numerous research studies. **The appeal of his four books,** The Tipping Point, Outliers, Blink and What the Dog Saw and Other Adventures lies in Gladwell's ability to collect interesting research and stories that highlight some of the findings of that research. **Some would argue** that his explanation of social phenomena is far too simplistic and, _because of this,_ he has been severely criticised.

As a journalist, not an academic, he has been accused of treating serious subjects too lightly. **The worst feature of his writing,** his critics argue, is that he stretches the truth to get a story and, _therefore,_ is not to be taken too seriously. _Nevertheless,_ Gladwell's attractive and easy to read style has made his books extremely popular. _Even though_ his discussion of the unexpected implications of research in the social sciences should be treated with caution, the reader can see many aspects of his or her life in his books. _For example,_ in his book, Outliers, Gladwell examines why some people are successful and others not, given that their inherent talent may be similar. He attributes success to a combination of innate ability, being in the right place at the right time, and a willingness to stick at something for approximately 10,000 hours. **Despite criticism** of the authenticity of his work, his books have been enjoyed by millions _especially_ as they allow readers to see themselves in the anecdotes he describes.

key task words

see glossary pp. 44-47

- appreciate
- assess
- consider
- criticise
- evaluate
- appraise
- decide
- determine
- examine
- value

explaining

meaning:
making the reader understand something by giving reasons for both 'how' and 'why' things are as they are

sentence starters

There are several reasons for ……….

………. has multiple causes which include ……….

………. is like this because ……….

There are several aspects to the problem to be examined, especially ……….

Each part of the problem contributes to ……….

Whilst A allows us to identify the cause/s of the problem, B enables us to ……….

The factors that contribute to this situation include ……….

The main effect of ………. is ……….

They are most likely to occur where ……….

As a result of ………. several unforeseen events have occurred, including ……….

The current situation exists because ……….

………. are usually caused when/by ……….

The main reason that ………. occurs is ……….

Other factors which enable this phenomenon to be explained, include ……….

There is no apparent reason why ………. is like it is; however, ……….

The reason for this situation is not clear; however, ……….

………. works by ……….

To put it simply, ………. is/are caused by ……….

The issue has had an impact on ……….

This has happened because ……….

If ………. were to change, then ………. would happen.

This event happens rarely/frequently/occasionally/on a regular basis because ……….

linking words and phrases

also affect	due to these	now that	so	this is how
and so	factors			
and this leads to	for this reason	provided that	so that	this is why
as a result of	from this/these/	resulting in	the effect of	thus
	that			
because	hence	results	the reason for	unless
consequently	if ... then	results from	then	when ... then
contributed to	it follows that	since	therefore	which is caused by

example

A monsoon is a seasonal change in the direction of the prevailing wind. Many parts of the world experience monsoons. The most famous are the Asian monsoons, but monsoons *also affect* parts of Africa and Australia.

To put it simply, monsoons occur *because* the land and sea heat up and cool down at different rates. **They are most likely to occur in areas where** a large continental land mass meets a major ocean basin. During early summer land masses heat up more quickly than the oceans. The air above the land heats up quickly too and, *as a result,* rises in great convection currents. *For this reason,* the air pressure over the land is low. The air over the ocean is cooler, more humid and more dense *and so* areas of high pressure form over there.

The atmosphere tries to maintain a balance and, *therefore,* the air moves from the high to the low pressure as wind. *Thus,* during summer the air moves from the ocean to the land, bringing with it rainfall. The flow of air is maintained by cooler air from the upper atmosphere that sinks over the oceans. In the upper atmosphere, the rising air from over the land mass is drawn outward over the ocean. **The main effect** of this air movement is the creation of a large vertical circulation cell driven by energy from the sun.

key task words

see glossary pp. 44-47

- explain
- account for
- interpret
- justify
- examine
- discuss

generalising

meaning:
developing a broad statement that seems to be true in most situations or for most people; does not include details such as evidence or examples

mathematics meaning:
using particular examples to develop an equation or mathematical model to describe the overall situation

sentence starters

In the usual course of events ………,

In the vast majority of cases ………,

Whilst there are exceptions to the rule, for the most part ………. applies.

A number of general statements can be made about ……….

The following summary captures the essence of the problem/situation/character's motives, etc.

There are exceptions to this general trend, although, for the most part, ………. is relevant/evident/significant.

Generally speaking, ………. is relevant in this case.

In this instance, the general rule of ………. is significant.

To summarise, then, the following generalisations are apparent:

There are anomalies; however, a general pattern emerges which is ……….

In essence, the situation is thus:

………. is more usual than ……….

An examination of the data reveals several generalisations ……….

From the evidence, it is possible to suggest the following generalisation/s:

More general trends appear in the longer rather than the shorter term.

The general characteristics of ………. are ……….

The following photographs capture the essence of the topic.

The principle of ………. can be applied to ……….

………. is a broad statement which encompasses the essential elements of ……….

In a more general way, the ideas can be represented like this:

………. has the same general idea as ……….

linking words and phrases

as likely as not	for the most part	likely	most often	primarily
broadly speaking	generally	mainly	mostly	quintessential/ quintessentially
centrally	in common	many	normally	reasonably assumed
characteristically	in general	more likely than not	often	regularly
commonly	in most/a large number of cases	more often than not	on average	typically
essentially	in the main	most	on the whole	usually

example

In Great Britain, there is growing concern about the rising prevalence of childhood obesity — a trend that first emerged in the 1980s. Whilst the causal factors are not always clear or able to be isolated, **a number of general statements** can be made about this serious problem.

In the vast majority of cases, obesity is the direct result of an imbalance between the energy consumed and the energy expended. _Typically_, an obese child does not do enough to use the energy from his or her food intake. **There are exceptions to this;** children can be genetically predisposed to obesity. However, this of itself is insufficient to explain the worsening situation.

Generally speaking, several broad trends have emerged which have contributed to this problem. _By and large_, food is much cheaper in real terms now than a generation ago. Incomes have risen; in our 'time poor' world, takeaway and pre-prepared foods are consumed by _many_ in preference to home cooked meals. _In the main_, exercise is more expensive than previously, leading to a decrease in physical activity.

On the whole, energy intake has risen since the 1980s; incidental physical activity has declined; children spend more leisure time on activities associated with burgeoning technology; and advertising targets children with products that are high in energy but nutritionally poor.

key task words

see glossary pp. 44-47

- generalise
- summarise
- assess
- outline
- sketch
- abstract
- explain
- extend

inferring/ interpreting

meaning:

using what is provided to make meaning or arrive at an answer; to uncover the answer even though it is not directly said or stated

sentence starters

It can be inferred that ....

It means that ....

It is unclear what .... means, but a plausible explanation is ....

It is reasonable to assume that ....

Reading between the lines suggests that ....

My interpretation of .... is supported by ....

Whilst .... is commonly understood to mean ...., I think it means ....

There are several interpretations of the same event, but the most popular is ....

The answer to the question is not obvious, but I think ....

The texts say, '..........' and this means, ...

.... is how/why we know that ....

This interpretation is supported by the following evidence:

.... reveals a great deal about the character/situation/problem/topic.

It is likely that .... because ....

The illustration supports the information in the text by ....

Smith (2008) states .... and this directly supports the findings of Jones (2010), who notes ....

The graph/table shows .... and this could mean ....

The data reveals the following trends:

Even though it is not directly stated, it is apparent that ....

A common but incorrect interpretation is ....

.... has several possible interpretations; however, ... is the most likely.

linking words and phrases

although	consequently	hence	it is evident	since
and reveal	despite	however	it seems	the reason for
as a result	due to	in other words	may mean that	therefore
because	even though	it is clear	might mean	this is how
by contrast	evidently	it appears	results	this is why
clearly	far from	it can be inferred	revealed by	whereas

example

Statistics indicate that the United Kingdom has one of the lowest rates of gun homicide in the world. On average each year it records .23 intentional homicides per million residents. *In contrast*, South Africa has the highest gun homicide rate, with 700 homicides per million. **There are several interpretations that might explain this huge difference. It could mean** that in the UK gun ownership is more strictly controlled by law than in South Africa. *As a result*, potential criminals have much less easy access to firearms. **It is reasonable to assume that** these statistics *may also suggest* something about the effectiveness of law enforcement in the two countries. Finally, **this data reveals** a strong link between crime and the level of poverty in a country. South Africa has a much larger and poorer underclass than the UK. *Even though* South Africa has left behind the apartheid era, the inequalities that system created will take many years to overcome. Poor people in South Africa still have much less access to education and social services than in the UK. *It is evident* that in such a society poverty and violent crime go hand in hand.

Source: http://www.nationmaster.com/country-info/stats/Crime/Murders-with-firearms-per-million

key task words

see glossary pp. 44-47

- calculate
- determine
- extrapolate
- interpret
- infer
- assume
- conclude

justifying

meaning:

showing or proving that a decision, action or idea about something is reasonable or necessary by giving sound, logical and reasonable reasons for it; answers the question 'why'?

mathematics meaning:

giving all the logical reasons and/or mathematical arguments that have led to a decision

sentence starters

There are several/many reasons for ……….

On balance, the evidence supports the view/opinion/decision that ……….

The weight of evidence would suggest that ……….

Consequently, it would seem better to ………. because ……….

………. is a valid recommendation/suggestion based on ……….

There is, therefore, no doubt/some doubt/much doubt about ……….

………. is a better option because ……….

The reasons that support the choice of Option A are solid and based on factual evidence.

………. is a good idea because ……….

The best decision is ………. because ……….

………. is a reasonable course of action because ……….

………. is a necessary course of action because ……….

It is fact rather than opinion that supports the decision of ……….

………. shows an intelligent response to the problem/issue/topic of ……….

There are no valid reasons to support this conclusion.

Circumstances suggest the following course of action because ……….

The decision to ………. is an effective response to changing circumstances.

………. is well supported by the evidence which states that ……….

………. will prove to be the best decision in the long term because ……….

For now, ………. is the better choice of options because ……….

linking words and phrases

adds weight to	confirm/confirms	hence	is preferred because	substantiate/ substantiates
although	consequently	however	more than/less than	support/supports
as	corroborate/ corroborates	in order for	produce/produces	therefore
as a result	definitely	in spite of	prove/proves	under the circumstances
because	even though	in this situation	reinforce/reinforces	validate/validates
better/worse	greater/fewer	is inconclusive	show/shows	will ensure

example

Most cities around the world are facing traffic volumes that continue to put pressure on existing infrastructure. Motorists are becoming increasingly frustrated at the length of time it takes to travel even short distances, especially during peak hours. In response, many local authorities have decided to allocate a greater share of their budgets to the construction of bikeways. **This is an effective reaction to changing circumstances. There are several reasons why this is a far-sighted response to a worsening situation.** Many parts of a city are only accessible by road; _consequently_ commuters have no choice but to use their cars. Increasing the number of bikeways _will ensure_ greater access to more places; _therefore_ commuters will be encouraged to use bikes rather than motor vehicles.

Safety is a major concern and many cyclists state that they travel to work by car rather than by bike because they do not feel safe on their city's roads. Bikeways are safe ways and _this will lead to_ more commuters using bikes in preference to other forms of travel.

The construction of more bikeways is a necessary course of action given increased carbon emissions _as_ more and more motor vehicles use the roads. Moves to invest money in bikeways **will prove to be the best decision in the long term.**

key task words

see glossary pp. 44-47

- account for
- criticise
- extract
- justify
- prove
- verify
- argue
- defend
- support

27

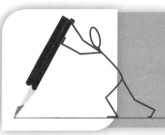

making recommendations

meaning:
suggesting a course of action for consideration by others; providing reasons (usually the findings of an investigation) in favour of the suggestion

sentence starters

It could be recommended that ……….

It would appear reasonable to conclude that ………., and therefore recommend ……….

In spite of ………., the best solution is ……….

Based on the findings, the following recommendations are put forward for discussion:

There are too many problems associated with ……….; therefore, ………. is recommended.

My recommendation, after looking at all the evidence, is ……….

It is, therefore, advisable to propose that ……….

The following recommendations, listed in order of priority, are put forward for consideration:

Based on the analysis of the situation, the following recommendations have emerged:

I recommend the following changes:

For the future, it is recommended that ……….

In light of the problem of ………., a suitable solution would include ……….

To achieve its goals, the organisation needs to ……….

The sensible option is to ……….

I confidently recommend ……….

The following recommendation should be enacted as soon as possible:

A list of the proposed recommendations with a summary of the reasons for each follows:

In the light of all available data, the proposed recommendation is ……….

There are a couple of recommendations from which to choose.

If the following recommendation/s is/are implemented, then the problem should be solved.

There are no guarantees that these recommendations will work; however, to do nothing may see the situation worsen.

linking words and phrases

accordingly	finally	in the end	moreover	to act upon
all things considered	general	in the final instance	on balance	to conclude then
as a result	hence	is desirable	so	to summarise then
because	however	is favoured	therefore	we can recommend
consequently	if … then	is recommended	these include	we can conclude
could/should/would	in summary	is valid	thus	will achieve

example

Preamble

Bullying at Anywhere High School has reached an intolerable level in recent years affecting many members of the school community. *As a result*, the school's administration commissioned a team of independent investigators to conduct a thorough examination of the bullying epidemic. Below is a summary of the recommendations presented in the report.

Recommendations

It is reasonable to conclude that the bullying situation at Anywhere High School cannot continue; *therefore*, **it is recommended** that the school develop and implement an anti-bullying policy immediately. **In light of the problem,** teachers need to be made more aware of the signs of bullying of children in their care. The current consequences for bullying are ineffective, *so* **in the future, it is proposed** that more serious measures are implemented to deter bullies. It is no longer the case that bullying occurs just within school hours. Cyber bullying is a huge problem; *hence*, **it is advisable** to involve all members of the community in the anti-bullying policy that the school develops. **There are no guarantees that these recommendations will work; however, to do nothing will almost certainly see the situation worsen.**

key task words

see glossary pp. 44-47

- present
- propose
- suggest
- recommend
- prepare
- construct
- devise

providing evidence

meaning:

referring to sources, illustrations and other evidence about something to support the points that have been made

sentence starters

Analysis of the data suggests ……….

The evidence clearly reveals ……….

The graph shows that ……….

It is clear from the table that ……….

As shown by the information in ……….,

Clear trends are evident between (date) and (date) and these are ……….

Should the trend continue, then by (date) it is projected that ……….

As seen in Diagram A, ……….

Table B shows ……….

According to the figures in Table A, ……….

The point is well supported by the available data.

Table A and B show conflicting information, viz., ……….

Compared with the data in Table A, the data in Table B shows ……….

………. can be supported by the information in Graph A .

This/these argument/s are confirmed by several authors including (author, date), who states that ……….

Popular opinion supports/does not support ……….

Over many years ………. has contributed to the body of knowledge about ……….

According to (author, date) who states that ……….,

(Author, date) argues that ………. and this is supported by (author, date).

Several authors (author 1: date, author 2: date, author 3: date) are in agreement about …..

Most experts agree/disagree ……….

The evidence collected allows the following observations to be made:

The evidence is very convincing because it is stated so clearly.

linking words and phrases

according to	closely	for this reason	indicates	shows
also	confirmed by	furthermore	it is clear that	such as
as well as	contradicts	illustrates	means	suggest/suggests
based on	evident/evidently	in addition to	moreover	support/supports
case in point	for example	in detail	refutes	through
clearly	for instance	indeed	reveals	viz.

example

Most historians agree that the aggressive foreign policies of Adolf Hitler and his Nazi regime were a major cause of World War Two. There are a few Nazi apologists who _contradict this standard interpretation_. **A review of the evidence** however suggests that their view is a distorted one. _For example_, in his 1924 autobiography, _Mein Kampf_, Hitler outlined his future plans for Europe. He wanted to destroy the Soviet Union and then planned to use that territory to create living space for what he believed was the German master race. At the heart of his ideas was his belief in the importance of brutal struggle. **This attitude is illustrated clearly** in his declaration that "he who wants to live must fight". _In contrast_, "he who does not want to fight," he argued, "has no right to exist". _Furthermore_, in a 1928 speech Hitler emphasised the need to "destroy people's pitiable belief in possibilities such as world peace … and international cooperation". **This evidence clearly reveals** that war, not peace, was at the heart of Hitler's ideas. _What is more_, he never deviated from these core beliefs right up until his death in 1945.

key task words

see glossary pp. 44-47

- demonstrate
- expound
- extrapolate
- identify
- illustrate/exemplify
- prove
- refer

sequencing

sentence starters

Before beginning, it is necessary to ……….

Initially, check that you have ……….

The first event that happened was ……….

This is/was closely followed by ……….

After a significant period of time had/has elapsed, ……….

Once the ………. has been established/put in place/decided, then ……….

When you have done ………., then you should ……….

The second/next step involves/involved ……….

The next logical step is to ……….

Much later on in the story, it became apparent that ……….

Several days/months/years later, ………. took place.

A great deal happened before/after ……….

There is a defined sequence of events that should be adhered to.

It matters/does not matter if ………. occurs first.

After a significant amount of time, ………. occurred.

At a much earlier/later time, ……….

The key events in the order in which they happened are listed below:

It is important that these steps occur in the prescribed order.

Meanwhile, there were several events happening behind the scenes.

It is hard to decide which came first, ………. or ……….

In the next stage of the construction process ……….

During the first stage of ………. the following event/events happened/occurred:

linking words and phrases

after	as soon as	first, second, third, etc.	lastly	previously
also	at the outset	following/followed by	meanwhile	prior to
and then (use sparingly)	at the same time	formerly	moreover	subsequently
as	before	initially	now that	the next day/week/year
as a final point	every time	in summary	once	ultimately
as well as	finally	in the beginning	on top of	up until now

example

The Romans were remarkable in many ways; of particular note is the way in which they built roads. These structures have endured for centuries _after_ their initial construction. Roman roads were built almost solely for the purpose of moving troops from one part of the Empire to another. **Before beginning,** the Romans mapped the shortest possible distance between the two points they wanted to connect. **Roman road building involved a defined sequence of events to which the Romans closely adhered. During the first stage** of road building, land was cleared of rocks and trees and _this was followed by_ the construction of a trench at the road site. **In the next stage of the construction process,** large stones were placed in the trench. _Once_ the foundation had been laid, smaller rocks, pebbles, sand and cement were placed _on top of_ the first layer. Broken tiles and cement formed the _next_ layer and interlocking paving stones were laid to form _the final_ and very flat surface. _Lastly,_ kerbstones were laid at the sides of the road and these held the road surface in place, _as well as_ providing channels for drainage purposes. The endurance of Roman roads in many parts of Europe is testimony to the **prescribed order of construction** which the road builders followed.

key task words

see glossary pp. 44-47

- outline
- trace
- summarise
- sequence
- order
- list

solving problems

sentence starters

The causes of the problem are many and varied.

This problem is one that is not easily solved because ....

The problem of .... has emerged over many years.

Recent times have seen an intensification of the problem of ....

The problem of .... has reached crisis proportions.

.... is an enduring problem in need of an urgent solution.

The problem has more to do with .... than the issue of ....

Whilst the causes of the problem of .... are unclear, the effects are widespread and persistent.

There are several causes of the problem of ....; therefore, a single solution will not suffice.

If we continue to ignore the causes of this problem, the long term effects will be devastating.

There are plenty of examples from which we can learn about the effective solutions to this problem.

In spite of ...., the best solution is ....

Solutions to the problem of .... have eluded us for many years.

Solution A offers several benefits in the short term, but fewer in the longer term.

Solution B is the preferred one because ....

The evidence is indisputable: solution A is the only choice.

There are too many problems associated with solution A, especially ....

There is very little evidence that .... has made/will make much difference.

If solution A does not work, then solution B should be tried.

Solutions in the past to the problem of .... have not tackled the root causes; therefore, the problem persists.

linking words and phrases

a solution is	clearly	has reached	should	to eliminate
and yet	despite	imminent	solution to	to overcome
as a result of	the effect of	multiple causes	solved by	to reduce
as there are	fosters/fostered	must	spawned	to succeed
because	gives/gave rise to	necessary	tackle the problem	urgent
caused by	grew out of	required	therefore	which leads to

example

Despite the fact that the homicide rate in America has remained reasonably constant for the past 30 years, **recent times have seen an intensification of the problem of** youth homicide, especially of inner city black youth between the ages of 13 and 19 years. **The problem has reached crisis proportions and solutions to date have not tackled the root causes.** There is very little evidence that tighter gun laws will make much difference, _as there are_ many parts of the country where gun ownership is more widespread, _and yet_ there is not a corresponding increase in youth homicide. **The problem has more to do with** the sense of alienation felt by inner city black youth _than_ the issue of gun ownership.

Black youths feel continually removed from the places in which they live; there is very little sense of community belonging, _which leads_ them to join gangs and often engage in drug-related violence. **The drug problem,** and its relationship to crime, **is an enduring one,** with evidence that addiction to popular crack cocaine _has spawned_ more aggressive and often violent behaviour. _Clearly,_ much more money needs to be spent on restoring hope for alienated black youth and providing them with a sense that they have a future. **If the causes of this problem continue to be ignored, then the long term effects will be devastating.**

key task words

see glossary pp. 44-47

- deduce
- investigate
- predict
- recommend
- suggest
- propose
- solve

summarising

meaning:

when something is summarised the main points are briefly stated in a short account and the details omitted

sentence starters

Thus, in summary, ...

Finally, ...

Generally, these key ideas emerge from the information ....

Clearly, it can be concluded that ....

The reasons for .... can be grouped into two categories:

The main points are as follows:

For the most part, ...

In the majority of cases, ...

All the evidence suggests ....

Let's review the main ideas thus: ....

The significant points that appear include ....

.... can be summarised in the following way/s:

So, to restate the opening remarks, the key ideas are ....

The five main ideas from the text are: ....

This information is useful for ...., but not so useful for ....

To summarise, then, the key points are:

The essence of the argument is ....

The essential ideas are summarised in the diagram below, viz., ...

From these details, a conclusion can be drawn.

The main ideas related to the topic of .... are ....

The central idea presented in this text is ....

The key features of .... are ....

Stated another way, the essential idea is ....

The amount of detail given makes it easy to overlook the key idea, which is ....

linking words and phrases

are as follows	firstly	in summary	on the whole	then
at a glance	generally	include/s	primarily	thus
crucially	hence	main/mainly	second/secondly	to begin with
essentially	in a nutshell	most importantly	states	to conclude
finally	in essence	normally	suggest/suggests	together
first of all	in most/many cases	often	summing up	to tie things up

example

Student absenteeism from school is a major problem that affects the education of a significant number of students. **The reasons for** absenteeism **can be grouped into two categories:** those that relate to the school environment and those that relate to the home environment. **In the majority of cases**, the school factors _include_ students' perceptions that the work is too difficult for them; real or imagined instances of bullying; and a dislike of certain teachers or subjects. _On the whole_, the factors that relate to the home environment _include_ the need for students to help at home, _more often than not_ with other children or an invalid parent. _In many cases_ of absenteeism, students have a strong attachment to home, _often_ reinforced by over-protective parents. **All the evidence suggests** that there is no simple explanation of the reasons for student absenteeism, as a number of factors combine to make this a complex problem. _However_, **one central idea emerges** from studies, and that is that the most important 'school factor' is the quality of the relationships between students and their teachers. **Clearly, it can be concluded** that this is an area where resources need to be directed.

key task words

see glossary pp. 44-47

- indicate
- outline
- sketch
- summarise
- paraphrase
- review
- synthesise
- conclude
- extract

synthesising

meaning:

to put together various elements (from several places or sources) to make a whole; the reassembled material is often original

sentence starters

The issue can be resolved by combining ………. with ……….

The investigation showed ………. and, as a result, ………. is a better alternative.

Research has enabled this conclusion to be reached.

An examination of the facts makes this the desired outcome.

All evidence and supporting documentation points to ……….

My recommendation, after examining all the evidence, is to ……….

New and unusual ideas for ………. include the following:

It is surprising that this idea/solution/point of view has not been seriously considered before.

The new design addresses some of the problems associated with previous models and, therefore, is an improved version.

There are several ways to resolve the issue of ……….

The new design brings together some of the best features of previous models.

The best features of ………. are ………. and the worst features of ………. include ……….. Therefore future models should include ………. and omit ……….

Improvements might include ……….

The information from Source A is different from Source B because ……….

The best solution to the problem is ………. because it takes into account information from several sources.

If money were not an issue, the model would include ……….

The elements of the design could be assembled in the following way:

Several sources have been used to create ……….

I have used elements of style from several places to design ……….

………. is an innovative use for a traditional object.

linking words and phrases

although	collectively	furthermore	instead of	therefore
and, as a result	combines	however	joins/joined	to blend the ideas
because	consequently	if … then	merge/d	together
but	drawn together	in order for	nevertheless	whereas
cause/caused	even though	in that respect	on the other hand	while
causes	exclude	include	so	whilst

example

School bags have come a long way in their design from the satchels of decades ago. Children have to carry much more to and from school than their parents and grandparents; _therefore_, bags should be chosen with care. **The 'Pack and Stack' carrier designed by Carryall Solutions Inc.** addresses some of the problems **associated with** other school bags and is, therefore, the most superior design to date. **The best features of existing models include** their ergonomic design; their compartments to hold a variety of luggage of all shapes and sizes; and the fact that they can be used both as a backpack and a case on wheels. _However_, with handles that adjust to only one height, existing models do not generally cater for the growth of children throughout the school year. _In contrast_, the 'Pack and Stack' has a handle with three adjustable positions. _Even though_ the fabric is fully waterproof (many existing models are showerproof), the weight of the school bag is not compromised. **If money were not an issue**, the 'Pack and Stack' would contain compartments with hard walls, _so_ that electronic devices are afforded a measure of protection from the heavy use of these bags by school students. **One of the worst features of existing models is** too many compartments _and, as a result_, the 'Pack and Stack' has reduced the number of these, _whilst_ making sure that they are all fit for purpose. **The new design brings together the best features** of existing school bags, with some clever modifications that make it one of the best on the market.

key task words

see glossary pp. 44-47

- construct
- extrapolate
- interpret
- predict
- synthesise

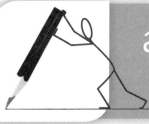

avoiding the use of 'I', 'me' and 'my'

explanation:

In most forms of formal, academic writing, the use of the **FIRST PERSON** (I, me or my) is generally discouraged. More authority is given to the work if it is written in the **THIRD PERSON**. In addition, the use of the **PASSIVE VOICE** (i.e., the 'doer' is removed) is also a prominent feature of more technical texts.

ways of saying

It could be suggested that ……….

This is/can be illustrated by ……….

It is seen through ……….

This is evident when ……….

Upon examination, it becomes apparent that ……….

The facts indicate that ……….

Popular opinion does/does not support ……….

This is exemplified by ……….

This illustrates that ……….

This shows that ……….

Therefore, it can be stated that ……….

Clearly, this becomes apparent when ……….

With some exceptions, sources generally agree that ……….

………. clearly points out that ……….

This is most obvious when ……….

It can, therefore, be perceived that ……….

There is evidence to support both opinions on this topic.

Smith (2010) is in total agreement/disagreement with Jones (2008) when ……….

Most notable exceptions to this rule are ……….

The author of this text believes that ……….

Observations reveal that ……….

avoiding the use of said

admitted	gasped	observed	shouted
agreed	giggled	offered	shrieked
announced	gulped	pleaded	sighed
answered	grunted	promised	smirked
argued	hissed	proposed	snapped
asked	mentioned	protested	sneered
babbled	inquired	queried	sobbed
began	insisted	questioned	spoke
blurted	interjected	quipped	sputtered
bragged	interrupted	quoted	stammered
called	jeered	ranted	stated
claimed	joked	reasoned	suggested
commented	laughed	reassured	taunted
complained	lied	remembered	teased
congratulated	mimicked	reminded	told
cried	moaned	repeated	urged
declared	mumbled	replied	uttered
denied	murmured	requested	vowed
dictated	muttered	retorted	whimpered
drawled	nagged	roared	whispered
exclaimed	noted	scolded	wondered
explained	objected	screamed	yelled

substitutes for 'says that'

explanation:

It is common practice in academic writing to cite (either directly or indirectly) authors who have written about the topic that you are currently studying. 'Smith says that ..., Peters says that ..., Chung says that ..., etc., can be very tedious and unsophisticated.

ways of saying

admits that

argues that

asserts that

comes to the conclusion that

concludes that

contradicts the commonly held beliefs

estimates that

explains in more detail

is in full agreement

makes it very clear that

offers a well-considered solution

offers an alternative explanation

pleads the case for

proposes a more viable solution

puts forward the view that

rejects all other alternatives

rejects the evidence that

reports the following findings

repudiates the arguments

stresses the point that

urges the reader to

vehemently denies

degrees of intensity (modality)

	least intense									most intense
certainty	never	scarce/scarcely	perhaps/in some cases	might	could	likely/as likely as not/in all likelihood	inevitable/inevitably	undoubted/undoubtedly	definite/definitely	positive/positively
confidence	outrageous/outrageously	suspect	unreasonable/unreasonably	doubtful/doubtfully	moderate/moderately	reasonable/reasonably	plausible/plausibly	undeniable/undeniably	irrefutable/irrefutably	unequivocal/unequivocally
emphasis	quite	simply	really	conceivable/conceivably	very	sure/surely	terrible/terribly	definite/definitely	incredible/incredibly	absolute/absolutely
extent	never	scarce/scarcely	limited	partly	general/generally	mainly	almost	complete/completely	conclusive/conclusively	absolute/absolutely
frequency	never	once	seldom	occasional/occasionally	sometimes	often	general/generally	usual/usually	regularly/in most cases	always
importance	desirable/desirably	prefer/preferably	require/required	integral	necessary	important/importantly	unquestionable/unquestionably	essential/essentially	mandated	vital/vitally
intensity	scarce/scarcely	slight/slightly	mild/mildly	intermittent/intermittently	moderate/moderately	typical/typically	incredible/incredibly	intense/intensely	unrelenting/unrelentingly	extreme/extremely
obligation	may/maybe	might	perhaps	could	supposed to	ought	should	have to	must	definite/definitely
probability	impossible/impossibly	improbable/improbably	potentially	perhaps	may/maybe	likely/in all likelihood	possible/possibly	probable/probably/highly probable	sure/surely	certain/certainly

key task word glossary

nb:

Use of the terms 'someone' and something' in these definitions is deliberate and is based on the definitions in the Collins Cobuild Dictionary. These words allow the key task words to be placed in context; something that is absent from conventional dictionaries. Whilst some readers may find the use of the words 'something' and 'someone' irritating, this practice is known to enhance students' understanding.

abstract	to create a general idea about something rather than one relating to a particular object, person or situation
account for	to give reasons for something and report on those reasons
account for (maths)	to report on; to try every possibility
analyse	to examine the parts of something in detail and discuss or interpret the relationship of the parts to each other and to the whole; may involve description, comparison, explanation, interpretation and critical comment
analyse (maths)	to use statistical methods to summarise, compare or infer something
appraise	to consider something or someone carefully and form an opinion about them
argue/persuade	to present one or both sides of an argument and use persuasive techniques to convince others that your opinion about something is the correct one
arrange	to place things into a particular position, often with a degree of order or precision
assess	to make a judgment about something based on its value or worth (may include quality, outcomes, results or size)
assume	to accept that something is true without necessarily confirming it or checking its validity
break down	to make a list of the separate parts of something
calculate	to ascertain or determine something from facts, figures or information
calculate (maths)	to obtain a result from given facts, data or other numeric information about something
categorise	to divide things or people into sets or say to which set they belong based on common criteria
classify	to group things with similarities in the same classes or categories; to defend the inclusion of similar things into these categories
comment on	to present your opinion about something
compare	to examine two or more things or people and note the ways in which they are similar **_AND_** different

key task word glossary

conclude	to draw together the main ideas of something and restate them in a succinct way, often as a decision; a conclusion may involve making recommendations for the future
consider	to give opinions in relation to the information you have been given about something or someone
consider (maths)	to ensure that your response refers to the particular information you have been given about something
construct	to make, build or put together items or arguments about something
contrast	to examine two or more things and focus on the differences
criticise	to make judgments about something or someone, giving details to support your views
decide	to choose something or someone based on a consideration of other possibilities
debate	to examine both sides of an issue about something and come to a conclusion - or leave the reader/listener the opportunity to come to a conclusion
deduce	to reach a conclusion about something based on evidence that is known to be true
defend	to argue in support of something
define	to show, describe or state clearly what something is and what its limits are
define (maths)	to give the meaning or precise description of the concept
demonstrate	to show something by example
describe	to give a detailed account of the properties/qualities/features or parts of something or someone
devise	to have an idea for something and design and plan it
differentiate	to recognise or show the differences between one thing or person and another
differentiate (maths)	to find a derivative
discriminate	to recognise that two things or people are different
distinguish	to draw attention to, and make note of, the distinct differences between things or people
discuss	to consider both sides of an issue about something, without necessarily coming to a conclusion
elaborate	to give more information or detail about something or someone
evaluate	to give a considered judgement about the value or worth of something or someone, and support it with evidence
evaluate (maths)	to find the exact value of something
examine	to look at something carefully, often for reasons 'how' or 'why' something may have happened
exemplify	to give more information or details about something
explain	to make the reader understand something by giving reasons for both 'how' and 'why' things are as they are
expound	to present a clear and convincing argument for a definite and detailed opinion about something
extend	to include or affect other people or things

key task word glossary

extract	to obtain information from a larger amount or source of information
extrapolate	to use known facts about something and use them as a basis for general statements about a situation or what is likely to happen in the future
extrapolate (maths)	to extend a graph to obtain additional values
generalise	to develop a broad statement that seems to be true in most situations or for most people; this does not include details such as evidence or examples
generalise (maths)	using particular examples of something to develop an equation or mathematical model to describe the overall situation
identify	to notice or discover the existence or presence of something or someone
illustrate	to use examples of something to give more detail to information or more weight to an argument
indicate	to point out something from available information
infer/interpret	to use what is provided to make meaning or arrive at an answer; to uncover the answer even though it is not directly said or stated
investigate	to examine the reasons for something
justify	to show or prove that a decision, action or idea about something is reasonable or necessary by giving sound, plausible and logical reasons for it; answers the question 'why'
justify (maths)	to give all the logical reasons and/or mathematical arguments that have led to a decision
list	arranging related items in order, usually under one another
order	to arrange things in a logical way
outline	to give all the main ideas about something without the details
paraphrase	to restate what someone has said or written in a slightly different way from the way it was first stated; the meaning is retained
predict	to suggest what might happen based on the available information
prepare	to gather what you need to make ready for something that is going to happen
present	to put forward something for consideration
propose	to put forward something (for example, a plan, an idea, a point of view, an argument, a suggestion, etc.)
prove	to support something with facts and figures
prove (maths)	to produce a logical mathematical argument that shows the truth of a statement for all values or situations
quote	to repeat words exactly as they appear in the material
recommend	to suggest a course of action for consideration by others; provide reasons (usually the findings of the investigation) in favour of the suggestion
refer	to use material in your answer without necessarily directly quoting from the stimulus material or information
review	to go back over earlier points about something, often with a view to what went wrong or could be improved

key task word glossary

sequence	to put things in the order in which things are arranged, actions are carried out, or events happen
sketch	to give the main ideas briefly about something or to create a sketch or drawing that shows the essential features; detail or accuracy is not required
solve	to find an answer or solution to a problem
suggest	to put forward or propose an idea or plan about something for someone to think about
support	to use a fact to support a statement or theory about something
summarise	to give a short account of something with the main points but not the details
synthesise	to put together various elements (from several places or sources) to make a whole; the reassembled material is often original
trace	to show how events/arguments progress and develop
value	to establish the worth of something or someone
verify	to back up a particular result and prove something
verify (maths)	to test the truth of something

my useful words and phrases

my useful words and phrases

about the author

Patricia Hipwell is an independent literacy consultant for her own company, **logonliteracy**. She delivers literacy professional development to teachers in Australia, and works predominantly in Queensland schools. Patricia has specialised in assisting all teachers to be literacy teachers, especially high school subject specialists who often struggle with what it means to be a content area teacher and a literacy teacher. Assessment has been an area of interest for many years and much of Patricia's work enables teachers to create assessment that is 'do-able'. Students often have very little idea of what they are required to do and rely heavily on parents/caregivers to assist them.

The idea for this book came from the author's experiences with her own children, especially Elizabeth, who is pursuing tertiary studies. Students struggle with putting into words what they want to say, especially when the 'saying' involves writing. It has been Patricia's experience that students need help to develop the language that mature writers use. In this book there are sentence starters and linking words and phrases that students should use when demonstrating a particular writing skill. Language is the way that it is because of the job that it does, and letting students into the secret of this makes a significant difference to the quality of the work they produce.

Patricia has developed a number of resources to assist students' literacy development. She is available to provide professional development to teachers to support the use of the resources, including this one, that she recommends. For further information, contact:

Patricia Hipwell

Mobile 0429727313 | email: pat.hipwell@gmail.com

Brisbane, Queensland 4075, Australia